Animal Teams

Dolphin Pods

by Laura Perdew

FOCUS READERS

BEACON

www.focusreaders.com

Focus Readers is distributed by North Star Editions:
sales@northstareditions.com | 888-417-0195

Produced for Focus Readers by Red Line Editorial.

Photographs ©: Shutterstock Images, cover, 1, 4, 6, 8, 10, 12, 17, 18, 20–21, 27, 29; iStockphoto, 14, 22, 24

Library of Congress Cataloging-in-Publication Data
Names: Perdew, Laura, author.
Title: Dolphin pods / by Laura Perdew.
Description: Mendota Heights, MN: Focus Readers, [2025] | Series: Animal teams | Includes bibliographical references and index. | Audience: Grades 2-3
Identifiers: LCCN 2024002700 (print) | LCCN 2024002701 (ebook) | ISBN 9798889981916 (hardcover) | ISBN 9798889982470 (paperback) | ISBN 9798889983569 (pdf) | ISBN 9798889983033 (ebook)
Subjects: LCSH: Dolphins--Juvenile literature. | Dolphins--Behavior--Juvenile literature. | Animal societies--Juvenile literature.
Classification: LCC QL737.C432 P454 2025 (print) | LCC QL737.C432 (ebook) | DDC 599.5315--dc23/eng/20240229
LC record available at https://lccn.loc.gov/2024002700
LC ebook record available at https://lccn.loc.gov/2024002701

Printed in the United States of America
Mankato, MN
082024

About the Author

Laura Perdew is an author coach, presenter, former teacher, and the author of more than 50 fiction and nonfiction books for kids. Her books highlight the wonders of nature and the environment, and call for action to preserve it. She lives in Boulder, Colorado.

Table of Contents

Chapter 1

Mud Rings

A dolphin **pod** swims in shallow water. The dolphins spot a school of fish. One dolphin swims in a circle around the fish. The dolphin beats its tail on the seafloor. Sand and mud swirl into a mud ring.

A school can include thousands of fish.

Dolphins usually swallow their prey whole.

The fish are stuck inside the ring of mud. The rest of the dolphins wait outside the ring.

The first dolphin tightens the circle. The fish inside feel trapped. They panic. They try to jump out of the ring to escape. But the other dolphins are ready. The fish jump into the dolphins' open mouths. The hunt is a success. The dolphins feast on their **prey**.

Dolphins come in many different sizes. The smallest kind is 4 feet (1.2 m) long. The largest is 30 feet (9.1 m) long.

Chapter 2

Living in Dolphin Pods

Dolphins are **social** animals. Most dolphins live in groups called pods. Being in pods helps keep them safe. Dolphins warn one another when **predators** are nearby. They hunt and play together, too.

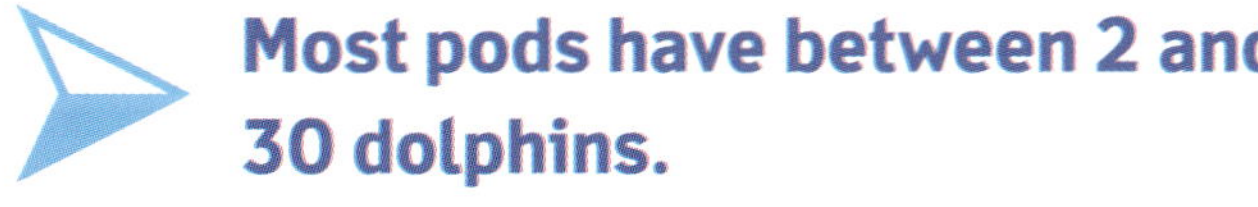
Most pods have between 2 and 30 dolphins.

A dolphin mother gives birth to one calf at a time.

There are three types of dolphin pods. One type is a nursery pod. In those pods, mothers and **calves** live together. When dolphin calves are born, they are not independent.

They need their mothers. So, calves often stay with their mothers for years. The mothers take care of the young. These pods use teamwork, too. For example, some mothers hunt while others watch the calves. And calves learn hunting skills from the adults.

Another kind of pod has only young dolphins. These juveniles have grown enough to leave their mothers. Joining a new pod helps keep them safe.

Spinner dolphins are one of the most social types of dolphin. They are rarely found alone.

The third type of pod is a group of adult males. These pods are small. They often have four dolphins or fewer. But the dolphins form strong bonds. They can stay together for up to 20 years. These male dolphins hunt together. They defend the areas where they live. And they look for **mates** together.

After dolphins mate, mothers give birth to calves. The calves start life in a nursery pod. Like all dolphins, they will be social their whole lives.

Sometimes dolphins form megapods. Those huge pods can include thousands of dolphins.

Chapter 3

Communicating

Dolphins in a pod need to **communicate** with one another. Communicating helps them bond. They use communication to hunt and play. It helps them watch for predators, too.

Dolphins often leap out of the water when playing. Bottlenose dolphins can jump higher than 15 feet (4.6 m).

Dolphins can communicate in a few ways. They often use sound. Dolphins can whistle, chirp, and click. Sometimes dolphins scream or squeak, too. When dolphins are young, they listen to others in their pod. They learn how to make different sounds. Later, they try out the sounds.

Each dolphin sound has a different meaning. For example, some sounds can show that a dolphin is happy. Some sounds

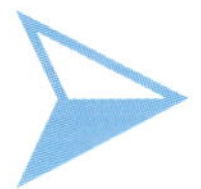

Sound helps dolphins communicate in dark, cloudy water.

can mean that danger is nearby. That way, pod members know to watch out. Other sounds are useful during hunts. Dolphins can tell one another where to find food.

Dolphins may touch fins to show that they feel happy.

Each dolphin in a pod has its own sound, too. The sound is called a signature whistle. Mothers and calves often use their signature whistles. The sounds can be helpful if the pair gets separated.

Dolphins also use body language to communicate. They touch one another. They leap and splash together. They slap their fins on the water. These actions can mean many things. Some show that danger is nearby. Or they can mean a dolphin wants to play.

Orcas are a type of dolphin. Each orca pod has its own way of communicating.

THAT'S AMAZING!

Big Brains

Dolphins are one of the smartest animals on Earth. They learn new skills quickly. They use those new skills for different tasks. Dolphins have good memories, too. These traits make dolphins great problem-solvers.

Being smart also helps dolphins work together. Adults can teach younger dolphins what to do. The group can plan actions together. And dolphins can care for one another. Their big brains help them raise young and stay safe. Pods even take care of sick or injured dolphins.

Dolphins can remember one another after 20 years apart.

Chapter 4

Hunting Together

Dolphins are **carnivores**. They eat many kinds of sea life. Fish are common prey. Some dolphins eat squid, jellyfish, shrimp, and octopuses. Larger dolphins may also eat birds, seals, and turtles.

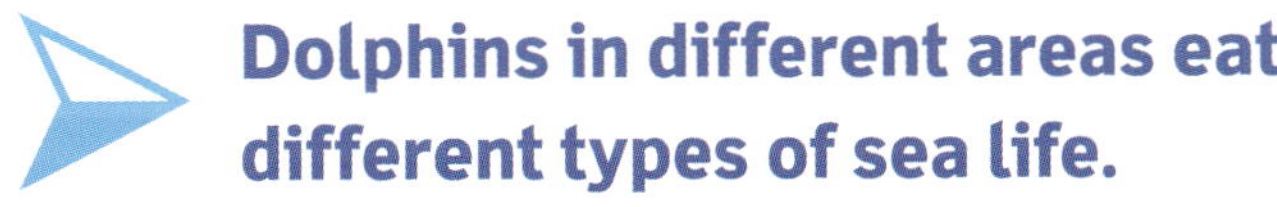

Dolphins in different areas eat different types of sea life.

Dolphins may chase their prey. Some dolphins can swim at speeds of 30 miles per hour (48 km/h).

Dolphins often hunt as a team. Creating mud rings is one method. Other times, pods **herd** fish in deep water. They force the fish into a tight ball. Then, dolphins take turns rushing through the group to eat.

Dolphins may also herd fish into shallow water. A few pod members eat. The others keep the fish from escaping.

Some pods use the water's edge to catch fish. The dolphins chase fish onto the beach. The fish can't swim away. Dolphins grab them. Then the dolphins squirm back out into the water.

In other hunts, dolphins slap their tails on the water. This shocks the fish. It may force fish into the air.

Those fish fall into the dolphins' open mouths.

Dolphins also use tools to find food. Dolphins often poke the seafloor as they search. However, doing that can hurt their noses. So, some female dolphins carry sea sponges. The sponges protect their noses. Dolphins use the sponges

Some dolphins eat up to 55 pounds (25 kg) of food every day.

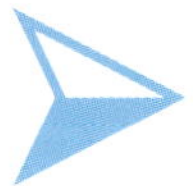

Female bottlenose dolphins in Shark Bay, Australia, are known to use sponges as tools.

to help them dig, too. Adult dolphins teach these tricks to their daughters. The young ones can learn to hunt for themselves. Later, they can help their pods thrive.

FOCUS ON

Dolphin Pods

Write your answers on a separate piece of paper.

1. Write a letter to a friend describing how being in a pod helps a dolphin.
2. What do you think is the most useful part of living in a pod? Why?
3. Which type of pod is made up of mother dolphins and their calves?
   - A. nursery pod
   - B. young dolphin pod
   - C. adult male pod
4. What might happen to a dolphin that is not in a pod?
   - A. It might not have help hunting for food.
   - B. It might not know what to eat.
   - C. It might have more food for itself.

5. What does **juveniles** mean in this book?

Another kind of pod has only young dolphins. These ***juveniles*** *have grown enough to leave their mothers.*

A. old dolphins
B. sick dolphins
C. young dolphins

6. What does **independent** mean in this book?

When dolphin calves are born, they are not ***independent****. They need their mothers. So, calves often stay with their mothers for years.*

A. newborn babies
B. able to survive alone
C. very fast swimmers

Answer key on page 32.

Glossary

calves
Young dolphins.

carnivores
Animals that eat meat.

communicate
To send and receive messages or information.

herd
To move animals together into a tight group.

mates
Partners that have babies together.

pod
A group of dolphins.

predators
Animals that hunt other animals for food.

prey
Animals that are hunted and eaten by other animals.

social
Likely to spend time with other animals of the same type.

To Learn More

BOOKS

Amin, Anita Nahta. *Is It a Dolphin or a Porpoise?* North Mankato, MN: Capstone, 2022.

Murray, Julie. *Dolphins*. Minneapolis: Abdo Publishing, 2020.

Vanden Branden, Claire. *Pink Dolphins*. North Mankato, MN: Capstone, 2020.

NOTE TO EDUCATORS

Visit **www.focusreaders.com** to find lesson plans, activities, links, and other resources related to this title.

Index

Answer Key: 1. Answers will vary; **2.** Answers will vary; **3.** A; **4.** A; **5.** C; **6.** B